A Raft of Sea Otters

THE PLAYFUL LIFE OF A FURRY SURVIVOR

BY VICKI LEÓN

LONDON TOWN PRESS

The London Town *Wild Life* Series
Series Editor
Vicki León

A Raft of Sea Otters
Principal photographers
Richard Bucich and Jeff Foott

Additional photographers
Charles Bancroft; Batista-Moon Studio; Charles Deutsch; John
Gerlach; François Gohier; Richard Hansen; Stephen
Krasemann; George Lepp; Tom Mangelsen; Steve Rosenberg;
Roland Smith; Stouffer Productions; Doug Wechsler

London Town Press
P.O. Box 585
Montrose, California 91021
www.LondonTownPress.com

Book design by Christy Hale
10 9 8 7 6 5 4 3 2 1

Printed in Singapore

Distributed by Publishers Group West

Publisher's Cataloging-in-Publication Data
León, Vicki.
A raft of sea otters : the playful life of a furry survivor / Vicki
León ; photographs by Richard Bucich and Jeff Foott.—2nd ed.
p. cm. — (London Town wild life series)
Originally published: San Luis Obispo, CA : Blake Books
©1993
Summary: Describes the characteristics, behavior and habitats
of sea otters, in context of their rebound from near extinction.
Includes bibliographic references and index.
ISBN 0-9666490-4-4
1. Sea otter—Juvenile literature.   2. Otters—Juvenile literature.
[1. Sea otter. 2. Otters.] I. Bucich, Richard. II. Foott, Jeff.
III. Title. IV. Series.
QL737.C25 L46 2005
599.7695—dc22
2004117675

FRONT COVER: This female otter off the California coast is
descended from the tiny stock of animals that survived
extinction in the 1900s.

TITLE PAGE: Pink and scarred noses show that these female
otters have mated.

BACK COVER: Wrapped in kelp, a sea otter grooms, scrubbing
its cheeks and face. This type of energetic grooming is often
done after eating and before a nap.

Contents

▲ To rest or nap, sea otters wrap themselves in the blades of giant kelp. Anchoring to kelp keeps them from being disturbed by wind and waves.

Certain animals inspire our curiosity and love. Sea otters are like that. Perhaps it's their teddy-bear faces. Or maybe it's the sight of their small furry bodies, bobbing among the wave swells of the Pacific Ocean. The sea otter's playful ingenuity amuses us. Its remarkable return from near-extinction amazes us.

Sea otters live primarily on the Pacific ocean's surface, near the shore. That gives people on the west coast many chances to see them. We watch these marine mammals as they dive, eat, and raft in small groups. We even get to see these wild creatures at their most helpless, as they sleep.

This book provides a close-up look at the sea otter, *Enhydra lutris* (from its scientific name, "otter in water"). First we'll examine the southern population in California; later, we'll look at the larger northern populations in the Pacific Northwest, Canada, Alaska, and its islands. You'll also read about its fresh-water cousins, the river otters.

Although protected by the U.S. Endangered Species Act, the Marine Mammal Protection Act, and California state law, the southern sea otter population remains fragile. But more is at stake than a well-loved species. The health of the kelp forest and the ocean itself also depend on the survival of this keystone mammal.

Living among the waves

Sea otters in the wild spend their entire lives trying to stay warm. That's a challenging job in the unforgiving north Pacific, where water stays between 35 to 50 degrees. It's even harder for sea otters, who don't have an insulating layer of blubber, like seals and whales do. In salt water, sea otters lose heat 25 times faster than on dry land.

These plucky marine mammals have adapted in an unusual way. They're covered

◀ Sea otters often rest, groom, and play in groups called rafts. It is normal for these marine mammals to float on their backs.

▲ To keep front paws and hind flippers warm, otters hold them up, out of the chilly sea. Keeping them out of the water lets paws air-dry.

with fur—the thickest, softest, warmest fur imaginable. A human head might have up to 100,000 hairs. But a sea otter has up to one million hairs in the thickest part of its fur.

Up close, this bright-eyed animal looks like it's wearing a fur coat that's much too big. To survive, it needs to clean its coat constantly, an activity called grooming. Loose, flexible skin and fur let an otter get to all the hard-to-reach places—even its own back.

How can fur keep an otter warm in the cold ocean? Sea otter fur has two layers. By blowing air bubbles between the layers, the otter keeps water out of the underfur. This animal spends several hours a day grooming itself. First, it cleans its fur by rolling in the water. Then it fluff-dries the fur by blowing air into it. Air between the two layers of fur acts as insulation, as blubber does for a seal. Clean, dry fur warms the animal like a down comforter.

▲ After diving for a purple sea urchin in the kelp forest, an otter heads for the surface. The rock it carries will be used to open its prickly prey. The otter may carry other food items, tucked in the baggy folds of skin under each armpit. These pouches are the otter version of a backpack.

But a sea otter needs more than air-filled fur. It has a high metabolic rate and a body temperature of about 100 degrees Fahrenheit. To keep warm, it also needs calories. The first thing on every sea otter's to-do list is to hunt for food. A full-grown male may weigh 60 pounds; an average female, about 40 pounds. Every day, a sea otter must catch and consume one-fourth of its weight. That could mean 10 to 15 pounds of protein, not counting the shells!

▼ Otters use rocks as tools. They smash the softer undersides of urchins against the rock to get at the protein inside.

Sea otters never have to worry about dieting, or eating their vegetables. They go after more than 160 different food items, including abalone, many species of crabs, clams, sea urchins, fat innkeeper worms, chitons, mussels, scallops, limpets, sea stars, turban snails, octopus, rock oysters, barnacles, and sea cucumbers. They also enjoy seasonal prey, like spawning squid. At times, the sea otter's choice of seafood puts it into conflict with human beings who enjoy some of the same species.

When it comes to food, individual sea otters have strong likes and dislikes. One may prefer crabs and urchins. Another might live on worms and abalone. Researchers have found that some sea otters pass along their food preferences to their pups. By choosing different foods, sea otters can hunt in the same area at the same time. In this way, they also help keep prey populations in balance.

Sea otters find their food supply by diving down into the rich habitat called the kelp forest. Turban snails and other creatures often live on the long stipes, or stems, of kelp. An otter works its way down the stipe, picking off shells, crabs, and other delectables.

Deeper, on the rocky reef and the ocean floor, the sea otter finds more prey. If it's a difficult-to-move mollusk, like the abalone, the animal searches for a rock to bash it loose. It can take several dives and dozens of whacks with a rock to loosen a single abalone.

An otter's front paws look like furry mittens. But these strong and nimble paws have claws that extend and retract. The sea otter's hind feet resemble huge flippers with long webbed toes. Their feet are the reverse of ours: the otter's big toes are where our little toes would be.

Flexible as an eel, the sea otter swims as easily on its back as on its stomach. On the surface, it pedals its webbed hind feet like a bicycle in the water. To swim down to the ocean floor, it flaps its feet, thick tail, and strong hindquarters in a sideways motion. It may look comical, but the otter is fast and agile enough to beat seals, wolf eels, and other competitors to get its prey.

▶ To keep fur clean, California sea otters groom a lot—but mostly in the sea. At rare times, they groom on land. As this otter cleans and brushes its fur, you can see how big and loose its coat is.

▶ Sea otters often rest in this position, with front paws behind their heads. The pink scar on her nose shows this is a mature female.

▲ Using its belly as a picnic table, a sea otter feeds on clams, breaking the shells against a rock. Every so often, an otter rolls over to wash off the scraps from its chest. Small fishes and seagulls eat the leftovers.

Dives usually take 30 to 90 seconds. If it has to, an otter can stay under four or five minutes. Although able to dive hundreds of feet, most dives are much shallower. About five to 50 feet is typical.

This busy hunter collects various food items on one dive, then stows them in the baggy folds of skin between its chest and its arms. Believe it or not, the otter has room for two prickly sea urchins in there!

The sea otter is one of the few tool-using animals in the world. Once it has all the food it can carry, it heads topside, often dragging along a rock. At the surface, the sea otter rolls onto its back and lays its catch on the picnic table of its belly. Using the rock as an anvil, it smashes its crunchy prey.

Other times, a sea otter might bang one shell against another. Even when you can't see an otter offshore, you can often hear the sound it makes. It's a series of quick tap-tap-taps, a noise that carries over water.

When going after abalone, sea otters may use a rock as an underwater sledgehammer. Some tools become favorites, and are used more than once. In harbors and other areas affected by human pollution, sea otters may recycle discarded bottles or cans as tools.

Even while munching messy crabs or sea urchins, sea otters like to keep neat. Every now and then, they roll over in the water, washing scraps off their chests, all the while keeping head and paws dry. Dining otters are very popular with seagulls and small fishes, who often hang around to catch the scraps.

Foraging for food is hard work. Sea otters forage three times in the average 24-hour day.

Sunset doesn't stop them, either. Like cats, sea otters possess good night vision, thanks to crystals (called tapetum) located at the back of the retina. These crystals act like mirrors, letting the eyes gather what light is available in the murky water. A clear membrane protects their eyes from salt water.

These hunters don't rely solely on eyesight to catch food. With sensitive paws and long whiskers, sea otters can capture clams and other prey by feel alone.

If human beings had the energy of a sea otter, we could watch them working at night, enjoying a midnight meal by the light of the moon, perhaps.

"Years ago in France, I read of Jacques Cousteau's work with sea otters and I dreamed of working with them too. Now, each time I photograph sea otters, I feel a new sense of wonder at this resilient little animal."

—François Gohier, nature photographer

With its outer fur wet from a dive, a sea otter cracks a clam against a huge rock the otter hauled to the surface.

Furry survivors

Millions of years ago, a member of the weasel family found it easier to hunt in the sea than on the land. And so this small mammal entered the ocean, becoming the ancestor of today's sea otter. For a very long time, the sea otter frolicked along the Pacific coast of North America. Eventually, its territory ranged from Baja California in Mexico north to Canada, Alaska, the Aleutian Islands, the Russian peninsula of Kamchatka, and west to the Kuril Islands of Japan.

◄ After a meal, an otter cleans its paws. This otter wears two tags. The pink one shows the area where it was tagged. The silver tag on the hind flipper identifies that particular otter.

For 8,000 years or more, sea otters lived alongside various coastal tribes. Human beings and otters shared the shoreline resources of shellfish. Otters were hunted for furs, but not in great numbers. Back then, there may have been as many as one million sea otters in the world.

That world changed forever in 1741, when a Russian fur-hunting expedition found the Commander and Aleutian Islands.

As soon as the cloud-soft otter pelts reached Russia, they caused a sensation. That began the first wave of death for otters.

Thirty-five years later, after Captain

▲ When sea otters raft, they sometimes rest head to toe. Sea otters in the wild live ten to fifteen years.

James Cook's exploration of the Pacific, Europeans saw otter pelts for the first time. Greed for the glorious furs started another wave of demand.

Sea otters don't molt like other furred animals, so their coats stay in prime shape all year around. Before long, frenzied hunters from Russia, Europe, and the United States had reduced sea otter populations to a handful.

In 1911, the United States and three other countries signed a treaty protecting the sea otter. By then many believed there were no animals left to protect.

But the unsinkable sea otter fooled everyone. Several tiny groups retreated to creeks in the Big Sur wilderness of coastal California. Further north, other remnant populations hid in remote Alaskan waters. Any human beings

aware of these otters kept the secret safe.

In 1938, a settler with a house at the mouth of Bixby Creek saw something unbelieveable. A raft of sea otters! Officials scoffed at his report, as did reporters. That same year, Highway One through Big Sur opened to road traffic, and the world learned of California's furry survivors. The slow comeback of the southern sea otter had begun.

▲ An otter can do a barrel roll in the sea without getting its head or paws wet. Otters roll and somersault to clean their fur, later blowing air into it. Air bubbles keep the inner fur from getting wet, so the otter's skin stays warm and dry.

Rafting in the kelp forest

◄The front paws of a sea otter are strong enough to handle rocks and yank mollusks from their hiding places. The paws are nimble too, able to pick turban snails off kelp as "fast food," or to catch prey in dark, murky waters by touch alone.

Like the word "flock" for birds, the word "raft" describes a group of sea otters. It's a good name. It conveys the Huck Finn quality of sea otter life: limitless, free, full of risk and joy in equal measure. Raft also echoes the Robinson Crusoe tenacity of this small animal that has returned from the brink of extinction once, only to be faced by new threats to its survival.

A raft or floating community in California waters may have as few as two otters—or as many as twenty or more.

Sea otters don't usually live or raft in the open ocean. Some animals prefer to raft in harbors and bays, like Monterey and Morro Bay. Many occupy the rocky nearshore habitat up to two miles from shore. Some animals collect in protected coves, like

◄Sea otters hunt and eat squid in the wild. Squid is also fed to captive otters that live in zoos and aquaria.

Point Lobos, or stay in a narrow arm of the sea, like Elkhorn Slough.

Other animals choose areas where the giant kelp grows. Below the ocean's surface exists a glorious dancing forest of kelp plants, 80 to 100 feet tall. Captain Jacques Cousteau, one of the ocean's most famous explorers and defenders, called the kelp forest "the sequoias of the sea."

Giant kelp has long, flat caramel-colored leaves, called blades or fronds. On the ocean's surface they form a loose net or canopy in the water, calming the wave action. Kelp is used as an anchor by sea otters, who grab one end and roll themselves up like a burrito. Wrapped in kelp, otters can sleep without being pushed around by wind or waves.

Giant kelp doesn't have roots. Instead, it attaches to rocks on the ocean floor with strong filaments called holdfasts. The kelp grows from the holdfast as much as a foot per day. Buoyed by hollow balloon-shaped bulbs on the stems, this plant grows toward sunlight, the ceiling of its world. After six months of furious growth, kelp blades die

and fall off, like the leaves of a deciduous tree on land.

The sea otter isn't alone in calling the kelp forest home. A great number of living creatures use it as nursery, food supply, refuge, and hunting ground. Over 30 species of fishes, 80 kinds of algae, and more than 300 sorts of invertebrates, from sea stars to abalone, take shelter and raise families here.

A kelp forest is one of the most productive ecosystems on our planet. It can support up to 300 pounds of fish per acre—three times the amount of fish that can live in ocean waters without kelp forests.

Sea otters do much of their hunting in the kelp forest. One of their favorite foods is that prickly fellow, the sea urchin— whose own favorite food happens to be kelp. By eating large quantities of urchins, otters help perform a valuable service. In the waters off southern California, where sea otters have disappeared, kelp forests have

vanished too. Armies of purple sea urchins have chewed them up. In Alaskan waters where sea otters feed on urchins, the kelp forests have come back to life.

For all the work the sea otter does, this marine mammal looks like the most carefree animal on earth. While rafting, sea otters rest or nap on their backs, legs stretched out, hind flippers crossed in the air. They often put their front paws behind their heads. Or hold their paws up in the air. Some otters cover their eyes with their paws.

Even though they look adorable, sea otters adopt these rest positions for a serious reason: to regulate heat. Paws and hind flippers are the only body parts without fur insulation. Keeping them dry saves energy.

Sea otters hunt, then eat, three times a day. Afterward, they groom with gusto. Rubbing their faces with their paws, they

"The welfare of the animal remains the most important thing for me. My relationship with wildlife is one of mutual respect."
—Jeff Foott, wilderness photographer

Two otters, fast asleep. Notice their long whiskers. When sea otters hunt, whiskers help them find prey, even in the dark.

▶ Southern sea otters spend most of their lives in the sea. Once in awhile, they come ashore to rest on rocks or remote California beaches. This behavior is called hauling out. Human beings lucky enough to see a sea otter on land should not approach it. That would disturb the animal, causing it to run away.

roll to get air bubbles into their fur, then shake their bodies like dogs do, leaving their fur almost dry. They follow this activity with a nap, usually with other otters. Most females, with or without pups, raft with other females. Males generally raft together. Sometimes, a male otter will maintain his own territory, rafting alone.

Sea otters communicate with a number of vocalizations. When they eat, they sometimes coo or grunt if the food is good—just like human beings! Otters growl, hiss, moan, whistle, chirp, and bark. We are still trying to learn what these sounds mean.

These marine mammals seem to have a good sense of smell. In the wild, when an otter approaches a group of its own kind, it jerks its head a certain way, then sniffs the other otters. This might mean "Hello,

I'm friendly."

These animals can't resist being playful. In the spirit of mischief, a lone otter might wake up a whole raft of snoozing otters by splashing them.

Curious by nature, otters sometimes raft or play close to humans. They borrow gear from divers and even jump into kayaks or boats. Male otters tend to play the hardest. Juvenile males often chase each other, wrestle, explore, and engage in mock bites and battles.

Sea otter migration is a mystery. Biologists are attempting to solve it by tracking animals with radio telemetry. They've learned that sea otters tend to have home territories, but may move seasonally. Males generally travel more than females. Newly independent otters often leave their mothers and may travel many miles away.

Mating & motherhood

Male and female sea otters don't have permanent mates. Instead, they join together for brief intervals.

When a male approaches a female, she soon lets him know if she's ready to mate. If not, she hisses and slaps him away. If the female is willing, the two otters braid their bodies together as they roll, over and over, on the ocean's surface. Gradually the male loses his gentle ways. As mating continues, the male sometimes pulls the female's head back, biting her nose. It looks cruel, as mating among wild creatures often does.

For one to ten days, the two stay together, eating, resting, and mating. Eventually

◀ Five southern sea otters raft and play together near a boat dock, delighting onlookers. But their fearlessness makes these mammals more vulnerable to people who harass or harm otters.

the female, her nose scarred and bloodied, leaves the male to rejoin her raft. He returns to his own favored territory.

Both male and female sea otters have alert black eyes, long whiskers, and thick fur. But females that have mated are easy to spot because of their pink and scarred noses.

Southern sea otters spend almost every moment of their lives in the sea. On rare occasions, individuals may come ashore on a remote beach or rock. This activity is called hauling out. Females sometimes do this, it's thought, to get away from males who want to mate.

Except for mating, males and females don't interact much. Sea otter fathers play no part in raising pups. That task is left to

▲ Sea otters have personality. Many have whiskers, markings, or fur color that make them stand out, like these two. As otters get older, they may become gray or white on the head or chest.

29

Juvenile otters can't resist toys.
Sometimes the toys are equipment
belonging to divers, like this inflatable
raft in Monterey Bay.

"Sea otters are a lot like people. The ones that are the most trusting end up risking the most."
—Richard Bucich, wildlife photographer

► An otter pup requires lots of care, and mothers lavish affection on them, even when they are big. Pups are dependent for as long as nine months.

► At birth, pups know how to hold up their paws and keep them dry. But the mother otter teaches her pup to dive, groom, catch prey, and other skills.

the female, who deserves a Mom of the Year award for her devotion.

A sea otter's pregnancy lasts about six months. The female gives birth to one pup at a time. In the rare event of twins, the mother cannot care for two babies, so one is always abandoned.

With southern sea otters, birth usually occurs in the water. In Alaska, it can happen on an ice floe. Immediately, the mother cleans her floppy pup, which has blue eyes at birth and is about two feet long. It may take an hour to get it clean, warm, and dry. Then the mother places the pup on her nipples, far down her body. In its first

weeks, the pup sleeps most of the time, even while its mother grooms it.

Sea otter babies know how to nurse at birth, and how to keep their paws dry. They also have a safety feature. Their downy fur is extra buoyant, keeping them afloat while mother forages for food below the sea. When left alone, the pup makes loud mewing cries. A mother otter can find her own pup, even over the noise of ocean waves and wind.

During the pup's early months, it lives mostly on her chest. An otter mother gets about as much rest as the average human mother—that is, almost none!

In the first months, a pup drinks its

mother's rich milk. Slowly she adds solid food to the pup's fare. The mother otter swims on her back, twisting her head so that one eye can scan underwater. When she finds a good spot, she leaves the pup and dives. When she comes up, she offers bites of her catch to the pup. Before long, baby is tearing into mom's favorite foods.

A sea otter pup's diet starts out crunchy, with crabs, snails, and clams. That's why it's born with a full set of 32 broad flat molars and sharp canine teeth. Even with teeth, pups often want their food already shelled. They will reject items until mother otter patiently prepares them.

Pups are born mimics. In a few months, most have mastered swimming and diving. This is challenging because a pup's fluffy fur makes it bob like a cork. Grooming and tool-using are its next lessons.

Up to three months of age, pups wear baby fur, the color of taffy. They are boisterous, often climbing over adult otters, or exploring mother's face.

As pups get bigger, their coats turn rich dark brown. Now they often nurse or rest at right angles to their mothers—and make a habit of stealing food from them. At six months, most pups can catch their own prey. Making a meal out of it is tougher. It

▲ Even after pups learn to forage, they beg food from their mothers. This pup, peeking through the kelp, wants the crab its mom has just caught. A seasonal food, this pelagic red crab comes from the open ocean.

can be painful, dealing with pinching crabs and slippery octopuses. Some pups still find it easier to swipe dinner from mom.

Mothers with pups often raft together. The older pups readily get into mischief, and will tumble younger otters, using them as toys until their mothers snap at them. Play between juveniles can get wild. They break things and make noise. When misbehavior continues, a mother loses patience. Grabbing her youngster by the

▶Protective mother otters clasp their pups tightly. A female otter may bear up to 12 pups in her life.

◀Pups play with everything they find—from kelp to diving gear. Juveniles may even jump into boats.

neck, she tows it as she swims away.

Healthy females usually give birth once a year. A mother otter may have ten to twelve offspring in her lifetime of up to fifteen years. She weans her pup at nine months, sometimes earlier.

If the pup is female, at three to five years it will reach sexual maturity, mate, and have offspring of its own. A male matures at around five years, but won't mate for several more years.

Given the time motherhood requires, it's no wonder that otters almost always give birth to one pup at a time. Yet despite a mother otter's devotion, death among pups can be high. For example, pups separated from their mothers during winter storms quickly die of exposure.

Still, motherhood is a skill and, over time, female otters get better at it. Biologists have found that older mothers lose fewer pups after weaning than younger ones.

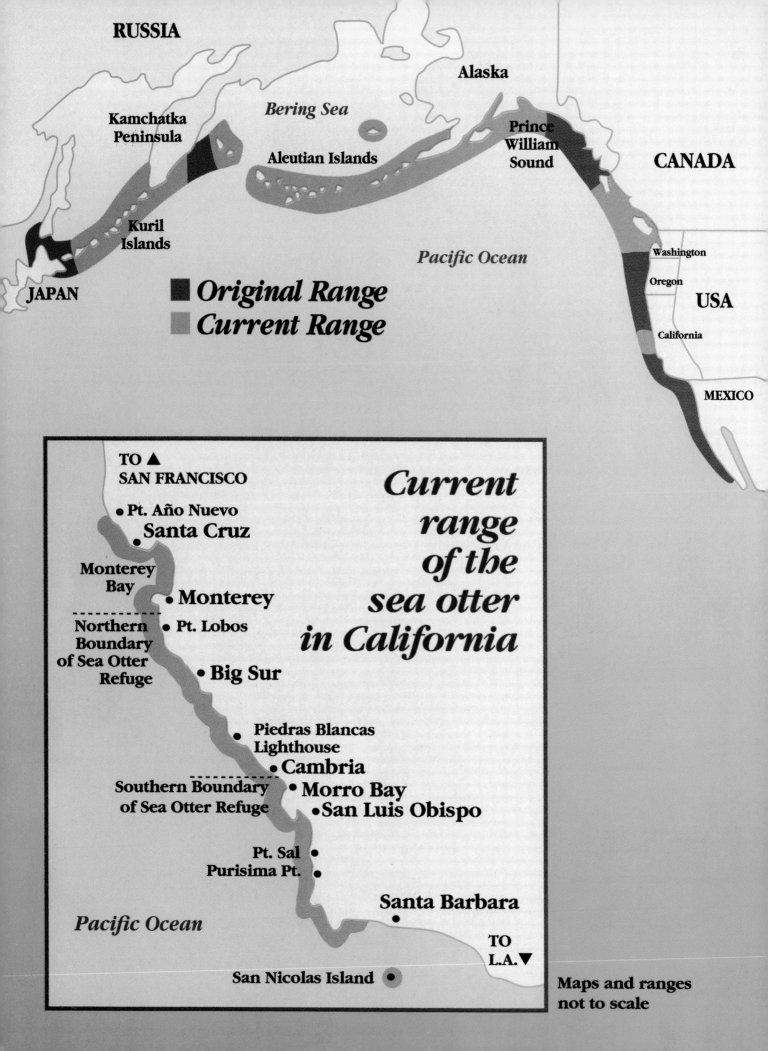

RUSSIA

Kamchatka
Peninsula

Bering Sea

Aleutian Islands

Alaska

Prince
William
Sound

CANADA

Kuril
Islands

Pacific Ocean

JAPAN

■ *Original Range*
■ *Current Range*

Washington

Oregon

USA

California

MEXICO

TO ▲
SAN FRANCISCO

• Pt. Año Nuevo
Santa Cruz

Monterey
Bay

• Monterey

Northern
Boundary
of Sea Otter
Refuge

• Pt. Lobos

● Big Sur

Piedras Blancas
Lighthouse
● Cambria

Southern Boundary
of Sea Otter Refuge

● Morro Bay
● San Luis Obispo

Pt. Sal ●
Purisima Pt. ●

Santa Barbara
●

Pacific Ocean

TO
L.A. ▼

*Current
range
of the
sea otter
in California*

San Nicolas Island ●

Maps and ranges
not to scale

A worldwide tour of otters

Biologists have divided sea otter populations into different subspecies: the southern sea otter *(Enhydra lutris nereis)*; the northern sea otter *(Enhydra lutris kenyoni)*; and the Russian sea otter *(Enhydra lutris lutris)*. These subspecies occupy different areas and don't interbreed with each other.

The southern subspecies, often called the California sea otter, lives along several hundred miles of central California coast.

The Russian sea otter makes its home off the Kamchatka peninsula in Russia and in the Japanese Kuril Islands.

Most of the large northern sea otter population lives in Alaska and its nearby islands. In an effort to increase sea otter numbers, biologists have tried translocation, or moving the animals to areas they originally occupied. Years ago, a number of northern sea otters were translocated from their Alaskan home to new colonies in British Columbia, Washington, and Oregon. In a similar program, southern sea otters were translocated to the Channel Islands off California.

Some of these colonies survived; others did not. What biologists have found is that it is not easy to move sea otters. During translocation, some animals died of stress or overheating. Others simply disappeared. Some otters swam back to where they were captured. This marine mammal, it appears, has a built-in compass. An otter

▼ When sea otters are orphaned or stranded and cannot be returned to the wild, they often find good homes in Pacific Coast aquaria, as these otters did.

▲ Alert to danger, a river otter stands on the riverbanks of its home. These fresh-water animals live on many continents and are more widespread than sea otters.

can find the same cove from which it was taken, no matter how far away.

Northern sea otters (including the translocated ones) look different from their California cousins. They're larger, heavier, and have thicker fur. A male may weigh up to 100 pounds. Alaska has less kelp forest habitat, so animals tend to raft in coves and bays. Groups or rafts of sea otters in Alaska can be huge—up to 200 animals.

The northern otters prefer to eat fish. They also haul out onto dry land more often.

The southern, northern, and Russian sea otters are members of the mustelid family that includes weasels, skunks, and badgers. But they have closer relatives, too. There are 13 species of otters world-wide, living around rivers and wetlands on every continent except Australia.

The only other ocean-goer is a tiny prawn-eating fellow called the sea cat. This rare species shelters in South American kelp forests off Peru and Chile.

River otters feed on fish and whatever else is in season, from water beetles and mussels to larger prey. In North America, river otters prefer frogs and birds. River otters living in Europe and Africa walk along river bottoms, feeling for fishes and turning over stones for smaller prey with their paws. Asian otters go for eels, rabbits, and waterfowl. In India and South America, fresh-water otters may hunt in groups, herding fishes toward the shallows.

Fresh-water otters give birth on land and can have up to four pups. At three months, pups learn to swim and dive. By four months, pups catch their own food.

Sleeker and more graceful on land than sea otters, river otters love to slide down mud banks and play together.

In earlier centuries, river otters were valued for their thick fur—but were otherwise considered pests. Once widespread across the U.S., they nearly went extinct in the early 20th century. Human beings trapped them, polluted their water, and destroyed 95% of their wetlands habitat. Today river otters have re-established themselves in Alaska and Louisiana, and are making a cautious comeback in about 20 states.

Largest of any otter species and a top predator, the giant river otter lives in rivers and oxbow lakes in the Amazon and other parts of South America. Males and females form mated pairs and live in dens, with up to seven family members.

Giant otters spend most of their day catching 8 to 12 pounds of catfish. They also enjoy eating piranhas. At times, these 70-pound otters fish in groups, bringing down smaller caimans (an alligator relative) and anaconda snakes, by attacking them on all sides. Sometimes caimans attack giant otters, who defend themselves by swimming under their attacker and biting its underbelly.

To rest, giant otters bask on logs near river banks. While in oxbow lakes, these animals make nests of floating grasses, where they relax and eat quantities of fishes.

But relaxation is hard to come by, even in the Amazon. Giant otters are territorial and have a strong desire for privacy. Human activity, such as boat traffic, forces them to retreat to remote rivers and oxbow lakes. Fossil fuels and mercury from gold mining pollute their waters. Although a protected species, their population isn't growing. Habitat loss greatly threatens their future.

▲ The Monterey Bay Aquarium pioneered an outstanding sea otter rehabilitation program. It has saved the lives of countless animals. Otters whose chances of survival in the wild are not good find a welcome at many aquaria.

► A month-old sea otter pup still wears the fluffy coat of a baby. It is at a rescue center in Alaska. Found with its fur soiled with oil, it was one of the victims of the huge spill at Prince William Sound in 1989.

Sea otters do have human friends on shore. Energetic groups like the Friends of the Sea Otter and Defenders of Wildlife, volunteers at places like the Marine Mammal Rescue Center, and aquaria like the Monterey Bay Aquarium help injured or abandoned sea otters. Some are rehabilitated and returned to the wild. Others find good homes in zoos and aquaria. Agencies like the California Department of Fish and Game and the U.S. Fish and Wildlife Service tag otters and track them via radio telemetry. Their mission is to help us learn what otters live on, die from, and most need.

These charismatic animals have a huge fan base, from school kids to teachers to Audubon groups. Many aquaria and museums in the United States and abroad display the animals and present programs on their value to the nearshore environment.

Laws have been passed, rescue plans developed, books written, and videos produced, all to educate the public and to protect sea otters.

But all these considerable efforts haven't solved the problem. The twice-yearly sea otter count in California has yet to reach the minimum number that biologists believe is needed to maintain a stable population. In Alaska, home to the largest group of sea otters, sea otter numbers have crashed in recent years. Other remnant populations show similar signs of distress.

Four factors make an uncertain future for sea otters.

Pollution. Pesticides, oil, and industrial waste find their way into oceans and rivers, harming sea otters. Oil may be the worst. Oil soils sea otter fur, destroying its insulating qualities, allowing cold water to

► Fish & Game professionals use a hand-held underwater trap to capture a southern sea otter. They use great care when catching the animals, to keep stress on the wildlife to a minimum.

▲ A captured sea otter is weighed and examined to learn its age, sex, and overall health.

▼ Tags help biologists track and follow California sea otters. Tags and tiny radio transmitters, implanted in some of the animals, supply important information about what sea otters need, where they feed, and how they live and die.

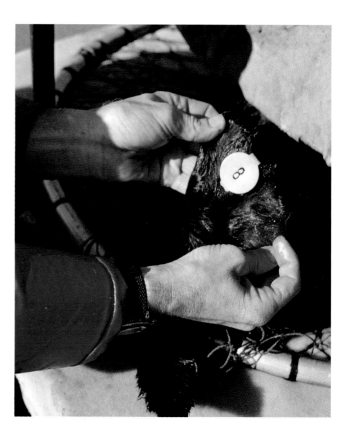

reach the skin. If this happens, the animal soon dies of cold. Otters groom, trying to lick off the toxic oil. When they do, they may die of liver and kidney damage. Thousands of otters died this way in the days following the Prince William spill in Alaska. Today, some shellfish in Prince William Sound are still contaminated with petroleum, causing sea otters who eat them to get sick or die. Besides the danger of new spills, oil may also reach otters when it is carelessly disposed of on land.

Population. More human beings join our planet each day. The California home of southern sea otters has more people than any other state. When wild coves become boat marinas, sea otter habitat may be lost. When commercial fishermen and dive

▲ Tagged sea otters are returned to the sea as soon as possible. Once they're released, biologists monitor the otters daily for movement, location, and foraging behaviors.

fisheries compete with sea otters for the same shellfish species, the animals' food supply is threatened.

Parasites. Many otters get diseases. In California, a leading cause of death is parasites, especially one called toxoplasma.

It's thought that otters get it by eating contaminated shellfish. The only animal known to shed the parasite in its feces is the household cat. When kitty litter or waste from thousands of cats goes into toilets, storm drains and streams, the parasite may end up in shellfish—and in sea otters.

Predators. Great white sharks and killer whales may be killing more sea otters than before. And even though protected, some sea otters still die from gunshot wounds.

For all the looking we do, much of sea otter life is still a mystery to us. But this time around, we owe it to the otters to protect them. In a world that gets more crowded every day, we need to leave room for other creatures. We need to leave resources for other creatures. Unlike human beings, sea otters can't switch to meat or vegetables if the food of the sea is gone.

These resilient marine mammals are a symbol of another resource we're blessed with: the Pacific Ocean. Otters, oceans, urchins, and kelp are all part of nature's great balancing act. By making the oceans safe for the precious few otters we have left, we also keep our watery planet alive and productive for all of us.

◄ Sea otters often let their paws cover their eyes while resting. This posture keeps paws warm and dry.

Sea Otter secrets

- Sea otters are the smallest marine mammals—and the only ones to live their entire lives on the sea without a protective layer of blubber.

- Some sea otters eat so many purple sea urchins in their lives that their teeth and bones turn a lovely shade of purple!

- Baby otters are born with a full set of 32 teeth, and can soon chomp through crab shells and sea urchins.

- Hunters once killed almost all sea otters for their fur. Their fine fur is twice as dense as any other furred mammal.

- Most animals can't live without fresh water. But the sea otter lives on salt water and eats shellfish, high in salt. Its powerful kidneys help get rid of excess salt.

- Every day, a sea otter has to hunt down and consume 25% of its weight in food.

- The sea otter is one of very few tool-using animals in the world. It uses rocks and shells as hammers.

- Sea otters help protect kelp forests by eating sea urchins. Sea urchins eat kelp. Too many urchins destroy kelp forests.

Glossary

Adaptation. Special body shape or behavior that helps an animal survive in its surroundings.

Buoyancy. The ability to float.

Canopy. Top layer of the kelp forest, floating near the surface of the ocean. Rainforests on land have canopies at the top of the trees.

Deciduous. Trees or plants that shed their leaves each year. In the sea, the giant kelp is also deciduous.

Enhydra lutris. The sea otter's scientific name. It means "otter in water."

Forage. To seek food or prey.

Grooming. To clean fur or feathers. Many animals and birds do this.

Guard hairs. Long outer hairs of the sea otter's coat, covering the softer, denser underfur.

Hauling out. When a sea otter leaves the ocean and goes onto dry land. Rare among southern sea otters.

Invertebrate. Animal without a backbone, such as a sea urchin.

Keystone species. A species that plays a key role in keeping plants and animals of an ecosystem in balance. The sea otter is a keystone species.

Oxbow lake. A U-shaped lake, formed from an old river. A habitat of the giant river otter.

Parasite. A tiny creature, such as a tick or worm, living in or on another animal and feeding on it.

Pelt. The hide or fur coat of an animal that has been killed.

Predator. An animal that hunts other animals for its food.

Prey. An animal that is hunted.

Raft. Name given to a group of sea otters that float, rest, and groom together.

Stipes. The long tough stems of the giant kelp.

Tapetum. Crystal layer at the back of sea otter eyes, giving it more visibility underwater.

Toxic, toxin. Poisonous; poison.

Translocation. To move wild animals from one area to another area they once occupied.

Wean, weaning. The stage when mammals finish nursing their young. Instead of mother's milk, sea otter pups move to a diet of solid foods.

About the author

Vicki León is the Series Editor for the London Town Wild Life series. She has written 29 books, including titles on seals, killer whales, wetlands, octopuses, and parrots in the wild.

Photographers

The work of 15 talented wildlife photographers appears on these pages. Principal photographers were Jeff Foott and Richard Bucich. The front cover closeup of a female sea otter is by Bucich. Back cover is by Tom Mangelsen.

Charles Bancroft, p.10; Batista-Moon Studio, p. 39; Richard Bucich, front cover, pp 11, 21, 26-27, 28, 30-31, 34, 35 left; Richard Bucich, courtesy Earthviews, p. 29 right;Charles Deutsch, pp 41, 43; Jeff Foott, pp 1, 6-7, 7, 8, 9, 12, 22-23, 24-25, 42 left, 42 right, 46-47; Jeff Foott/Bruce Coleman Inc, pp 18-19; John Gerlach/Animals Animals, p. 17; Francois Gohier, pp 14-15; Richard R. Hansen, pp 16, 29 left; Stephen Krasemann/DRK Photo, pp 32, 35 right; George Lepp, p. 23; Tom Mangelsen, back cover, p. 4; Steve Rosenberg, pp 20, 33; Roland Smith, pp 5, 40; Stouffer Productions/Animals Animals, p. 38; and Doug Wechsler/Animals Animals, p. 37.

Special thanks

- Michele Roest, Outreach & Education Specialist, Monterey Bay National Marine Sanctuary
- Mike Harris, sea otter biologist/environmental scientist for California Department of Fish & Game
- Rachel Saunders, Community & Public Relations, Monterey Bay National Marine Sanctuary
- Noah Hawthorne, giant otter researcher, Tambopata Reserve, Peru
- Richard R. Hansen, wildlife photographer & biologist

Where to view sea otters

Remember: all otters are protected species. Harassing or disturbing otters can cause them to lose their pups, or even die of stress.

- In the wild: in California, sea otters range from Marin County, north of San Francisco, to Santa Barbara County. Recommended spots: the highway bridge at Elkhorn Slough in Moss Landing; the great tidepool outside the Monterey Bay Aquarium; the Monterey harbor area; Pt. Lobos near Carmel; along the Big Sur coast; San Simeon Cove; along Moonstone Drive and near Cambria; the Cayucos pier; in and around Morro Bay.
- In captivity: over 40 aquaria and zoos worldwide have otters on display, including:
- Vancouver Aquarium, British Columbia; Seattle Aquarium, WA; Oregon Coast Aquarium, Newport, OR; San Francisco Zoo CA (river otters); Coyote Point Museum, San Mateo CA (river otters); Monterey Bay Aquarium, Monterey CA; Long Beach Aquarium of the Pacific, CA; Sea World, San Diego CA.

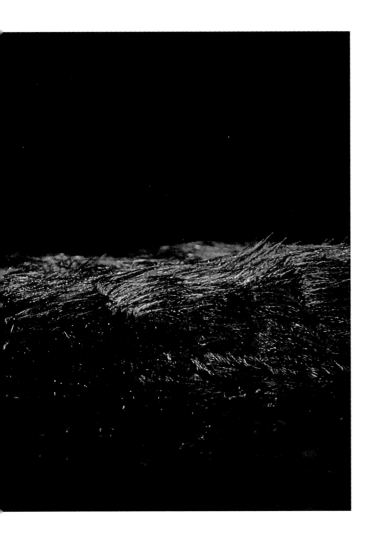

A sea otter is perfectly suited to its ocean environment. But pollution of its nearshore habitat makes the otter's future uncertain.

• Shedd Aquarium, Chicago IL; Philadelphia Zoo, PA (giant otters); Dallas World Aquarium, TX (river otters); Audubon Aquarium of the Americas, New Orleans LA; Aquarium for Wildlife Conservation, Brooklyn NY; Virginia Marine Science Museum, VA (river otters).
• Outside North America: Frankfort Zoo, Germany (giant otters); Blue Reef Aquaria, England; Osaka Aquarium, Japan (two species); National Aquarium, Canberra, Australia (Asian otters).

Helpful organizations and websites

• Monterey Bay Aquarium, 886 Cannery Row, Monterey CA. A superb aquarium and the world's most important center for sea otter research, rescue and rehabilitation. Their website is incredibly rich and responsive. Live cameras, clips of otters and more.Untold resources for kids, teachers. Web: www.mbayaq.org
• Marine Mammal Center. Links to aquaria, helping agencies, and teacher resources. Web: www.marinemammalcenter.org
• Friends of the Sea Otter, 125 Ocean View Blvd #204, Pacific Grove CA 93950. First advocacy/education group to organize and lobby on otters' behalf; still going strong. Superb newsletter called The Raft. Web: www.seaotters.org
• The Otter Project, a very active membership non-profit, working to protect the sea otter. Web: www.otterproject.org
• Defenders of Wildlife, a national advocacy and education organization dedicated to saving native wildlife and habitats. Large range of programs and materials. Sponsors of Sea Otter Awareness Week. Excellent resources for kids and teachers on a rich website: www.defenders.org/wildlife/new/seaotters
• Elkhorn Slough nature preserve and wildlife area. Great place to see otters, birds in the wild. www.elkhornslough.org
• Monterey Bay National Marine Sanctuary. This huge protected stretch of California coast and nearshore contains most of the southern sea otter range. www.mbnms.nos.noaa.gov
• This zoo/aquarium portal has great features, including ways that kids can help save the giant river otter. www.Azasweb.com
• This portal has links to good sites for river otters, giant otters, and sea otters; video clips of otters in captivity. www.otternet.com

To learn more

• *Sea Otters,* by Glen Van Blaricom (Voyageur Press 2001).
• *The World of the Sea Otter,* by Stephani Paine; photos by Jeff Foott. (Sierra Club 1993). Out of print but recommended. Stirring photos by Foott, whose work is also central to this book.
• Video: "A Sea Otter Story—Warm Hearts and Cold Water." Nature/PBS 1994. 60 minutes.

Index